THE NATURE SERI

EDITED BY
ANNA BOTSFORD COMSTOCK

THE INSECT NOTEBOOK

BY

JAMES G. NEEDHAM

Professor of Entomology, Cornell University

With outlines of 60 common insects

Drawn by:

CORNELIA F. KEPHART

Librarian of the department of Entomology
Cornell University

THE COMSTOCK PUBLISHING COMPANY
ITHACA, NEW YORK

THIS EDITION PUBLISHED 2021
BY
LIVING BOOK PRESS IN ASSOCIATION WITH HEARTHROOM PRESS

ORIGINAL WORK PUBLISHED 1921
BY
THE COMSTOCK PUBLISHING COMPANY

FOR MORE INFORMATION, CONTACT:
HEARTHROOM PRESS
INFO@HEARTHROOMPRESS.COM

ISBN: 978-1-922634-39-9

A catalogue record for this
book is available from the
National Library of Australia

This notebook is planned to combine schoolroom work with some field observation. The schoolroom work outline is of two sorts: color work on the insect specimens, and observations on living insects kept in confinement.

For the *color work*, outline figures of some sixty common insects are provided. These have been drawn by Miss Cornelia F. Kephart. They represent not particular species, but typical forms selected from the common groups of insects. Only so much of form as is common to members of the group is drawn. It is the pupil's task, first to complete or correct the drawing, and then to add the color. This should be done carefully with a good specimen in hand.

For the records of *observations on the activities* of insects, 40 blanks are provided. These call for notes on the feeding, locomotion, resting, shelter-making, defensive and other activities of the insect selected for study. Such observations may be begun in the field, but they are best completed in the schoolroom, where close observation of details is possible under more favorable conditions of control. Insects are small enough to be kept easily, alive, in proper containers. It is the pupil's task to sit quietly by, and watch how the insects perform, and then to record in the blanks only what he has seen.

Six *life-history* blanks are added at the end for the use of any pupils who may have the industry and 'stickability' to rear some insects through their entire life cycle from the egg to the adult. If such be selected as are easily supplied with common food and have a brief life period, this is not a difficult task. Certain common garden insects, like the cabbage butterfly, or noxious household insects, like the mosquito, are most favorable.

The *field work* called for is not extensive. It is only such as will yield specimens for study, and opportunity for learning whence they come and how they congregate. The collecting may be done on class excursions, or it may be done individually by the pupils by the wayside or in their home gardens. Its purpose is that the pupils should know the place in nature of the insects studied. The assignment of field excursions should always be at the discretion of the teacher.

The Parts of an Insect – One should know in beginning the study of insects that they differ much from ourselves in structure. They wear their skeleton on the outside like armor. It is composed of a brownish horny substance known as *chitin*. It is made up in plates that completely incase the joints of the body and the appendages and that are movable upon each other.

This armor is so hard that it has to be shed a number of items to admit of growth. The insect grows to big for its coat of mail, splits it on the back, pulls out of it, casts it aside, and grows a new one.

Insects do not breathe through the mouth as we do; they breathe through minute paired openings known as spiracles that are located along the sides of the body. The principal parts of an insect body are those shown in the accompanying figure and named below.

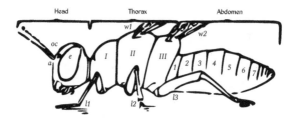

Fig. 1 Diagram showing the make-up of the body of an insect.

Head Bearing
{
Compound eyes (labeled *e* in the figure)
Simple eyes or ocelli (*oc*)
Antennae or feelers (*a*)
Mouth-parts - consisting of upper and lower lips with two pairs of jaws, swung from side to side, between them.
}

Thorax In 3 parts
{
I. Prothorax bearing forelegs (*lI*)
II. Mesothorax bearing middle legs (*l2*) and fore wings (*wI*)
III. Metathorax bearing hind legs (*l2*) and hind wings (*w2*)
}

Abdomen, composed of segments *1, 2, 3, 4*, etc.

4

The *life-history of an Insect* - One should know also something of the changes undergone by an insect in the course of its growing-up. The young of most insects are very different from the adults. The nine-spotted lady-bird beetle show in the figure, with hard shell and large wings that cover the body, is very different from the more worm-like, soft-skinned immature beetle shown beside it, the latter having no visible wings at all.

Fig. 2 A lady-bird beetle and its larva.

Insects differ greatly in the amount of divergence between young and adult forms. Those young that differ least from their adults have wings developing on the outside of the body and are commonly called *nymphs.* Examples of such are shown in plates I to IV. Those young that are more worm-like and that have the wings not visible externally during their period of growth, are called *larvae (*singular *larva).* Various forms of larvae are shown in plates IX to XII and XVI and XIX.

Fig. 3 A beetle pupa.

The differences between larva and adult are so great that there is always an intervening pupal stage. The pupa does not eat. It is a transitional stage only. It emerges from the last larval skin in some such form as that shown in the accompanying figure. It is usually sequestered in a silken or earthen cocoon or in some other shelter.

Out of a cleft in the back of the old pupal skin comes at length the winged adult insect.

How To Get Specimens Of Insects – Success in getting specimens for study is largely a matter of seizing the best opportunities that offer. Many insects come to us unbidden. Huge dragonflies and moths and beetles will sometimes fly in at open windows. Moths, caddisflies, stoneflies, mayflies, lace-wing flies, craneflies, and midges, and many beetles will fly to lights at night. They may be picked from a screen before a lighted window, or gathered up under a street lamp. Many kinds of insects are attracted to the flowers on the lawn. Some insects occur in swarms and are easily obtained in numbers at swarming time.

The most important single aid to collecting insects is a cyanide bottle. Insects placed in a bottle are quickly and quietly killed by the poisonous fumes. Many insects may be taken with a cyanide bottle alone, but for getting the swift-flying forms, a net is needed. Directions for making a both net and bottle will be found on the subsequent page.

How To Preserve Specimens – To preserve specimens of dried insects in paper envelopes costs nothing, requires no special equipment, takes little time and little room for storage, and yet yields a good material for color work indoors in winter. The envelopes used by entomologists are triangular (see figure 4 E). They are made as needed out of rectangles of blank paper. A piece, say post-card size (3x5 inches) is folded diagonally across the middle; one overlapping end is folded over and crimped by a cross fold of the tip. This makes the container into which the insect may be slipped as soon as killed. Then the other projecting flap is folded and crimped to close the envelope and name, date and locality are written upon the outside. Specimens so papered may be kept until needed in any tight (pest-proof) box. A few moth-balls or some flakes of naphthalene placed in the box may keep pests out even if the box is not air-tight.

The preparation of spread specimens for display requires more time and patience, and some special equipment. Insect pins and a spreading-board and proper insect boxes to hold the finished specimens will be needed. The pins will have to be, and the boards may be, bought from dealers.*

A good satisfactory *spreading-board* may be made from any smoothly planed piece of soft wood three-eights of an inch in thickness (a side piece from a cracker box will often be found suitable). Perforate the board with awl holes spaced far enough apart to accommodate spread specimens. Glue a strip of manila paper to the back of the spreading board.

To use this board, insert the insect pin through the body of the fresh specimen (or an old specimen that has been relaxed in a moist chamber) in the usual way.

Then turn the specimen upside down and insert the head of the pin into one of the holes of the board. Push the insect down against the board, spread its wings out flat in the desired position (hind margin of front wings in a straight line across) and, to hold them so, pin strips of paper to the board across them. Adjust also the antennae and legs and other appendages in the desired position, pinning them down under paper strips when necessary. Then place the board with spread specimens attached in a place where it will dry rapidly without molestation and leave it undisturbed until the specimens are thoroughly dry. If removed too soon the wings will droop.

Good insect boxes are expensive to buy and are not so easily provided; yet many a school has an attractive collection of local insects mounted in pest-proof, glass-topped boxes, made in its manual training department. Cigar boxes bottomed with cork, or with corrugated pasteboard, may be used temporarily to hold pinned specimens. The will serve until pests get inside, which will be longer or shorter time according to the fit of the lids or the efficiency of the repellents (moth-balls, etc.) kept inside.**

How To Keep Living Specimens Indoors – Aquatic insects may be kept in glass vessels containing water. – tumblers, fruit jars, battery jars, aquaria etc. according to size and number kept together. The climbing forms will need water weeds to climb on: the burrowers will need sand or mud to dig in: for some adult insects that might take wing and fly away a cover will be needed, but most aquatic insects are easily manageable.

Small leaf-eating insects may be kept and reared in jelly tumblers; larger ones in fruit jars. Keep lids on close, and change leaves as often as they become wilted and unfit for food. The work of procuring fresh leaves for forage may be allotted to one pupil each day, but each pupil should regularly clean and care for his own cages.

Cages of larger size may be quickly made by rolling cylinders of wire cloth, crimping together with folding-tongs the edges that meet, and covering the open ends of the cylinder with cheese-cloth. For ground insects one open end of the cylinder may be set down into a box of soil, and growing sods may thus be included in the cage.

Much of the best life-history work on insects has been done with apparatus such as this. In rearing insects it is not so much complicated apparatus, as careful attention that counts.

* Wards Natural Science Establishment, Rochester, N.Y. The Kny-Sheerer Co. 27th Street and 9th Ave New York, N.Y.

** A simple method commonly used in Switzerland for mounting insects for school collections will be found described on pp. 53-56 of Hodges *Nature Study and Life.*

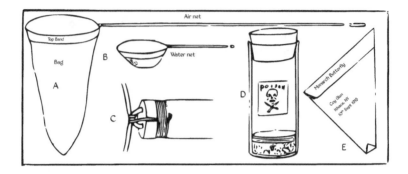

A and B, home-made insect nets. The rim is a circle of 9-gauge galvanized steel wire. 12 inches in diameter, with ends crossed and bent parallel. The handle is a light stick of wood 3 feet long with two holes bored in the end to receive the ends of the rim. The attachment of rim and handle is made by wrapping with 24 gauge copper wire, as indicated in C . The copper wire is first wrapped about the crossed rim-ends, then drawn down in two longitudinal grooves on opposite sides of the end, and finally the ends are twisted together securely. The top band is made of muslin, and the bag of the air net, 18-24 inches deep, is made of cheese cloth, bobbinet, or other netting, tapering somewhat to the bottom.

The water net is of like construction but much smaller (7 inches in diameter) and has a shallow bag, to facilitate the examination of specimens in its bottom when lifted from the water.

A cyanide bottle, D, may be made from any wide mouthed bottle by placing a little potassium cyanide in the bottom, covering it with sawdust or other good absorbent, pressing down on this a few discs of thick blotting paper freshly gummed at the edges, and affixing a "POISON" label.

Collecting envelopes, E, may be made as needed from a pocketful of paper slips of post-card size.

Inexpensive collecting nets may be purchased from the Simplex Net Co. Of Ithaca, N.Y.

A FEW GOOD BOOKS ON INSECTS

AMERICAN INSECTS. KELLOGG. HENRY HOLT AND CO.

ECONOMIC ENTEMOLOGY. SMITH. LIPPINCOTTS.

HANDBOOK OF NATURE-STUDY. COMSTOCK. COMSTOCK PUBLISHING CO.

INSECT BOOK. HOWARD. DOUBLEDAY PAGE AND CO.

INSECT LIFE. COMSTOCK. D. APPLETON AND CO.

INSECTS INJURIOUS TO THE HOUSEHOLD. HERRICK. MACMILLAN.

INSECT STORIES. KELLOGG. HENRY HOLT AND CO.

LIFE OF INLAND WATERS. NEEDHAM AND LLOYD. COMSTOCK PUB. CO.

MANUAL FOR THE STUDY OF INSECTS. COMSTOCK. COMSTOCK PUB. CO.

OUTDOOR STUDIES. NEEDHAM. AMERICAN BOOK CO.

INDEX TO INSECT NOTES

NAME OF INSECT   PAGE

....
....
....
....
....
....
....
....
....
....
....
....
....
....
....
....
....
....
....
....
....
....
....
....
....
....
....
....
....
....
....
....
....
....
....
....

INDEX TO INSECT NOTES

NAME OF INSECT   PAGE

NOTES ON INSECTS

NOTES ON LIVING INSECTS

Date: See picture, plate_____   Measurements:

Name of Insect: Length:

                                                Expanse:

(Underscore such words as apply)

I. Stages Found   Where Found   Number found together

     adult

     pups

     larva or nymph

     eggs

2. Feeding where

     on what

     in what manner

3. Moving about how (walking, swimming, flying etc).

Using what parts (legs, wings, tail, etc).

speed

directness

4. Resting where

    in what position

5. Shelter making (describe or sketch nest, burrow, web, cocoon, etc).

6. Enemies and means of defense.

7. Other activities.

Beneficial or injurious to man and why.

NOTES ON LIVING INSECTS

Date: See picture, plate_____   Measurements:

                                                          Length:
Name of Insect:

                                                          Expanse:

(Underscore such words as apply)

I. Stages Found   Where Found   Number found together

    adult

    pups

    larva or nymph

    eggs

2. Feeding where

    on what

    in what manner

3. Moving about how (walking, swimming, flying etc).

Using what parts (legs, wings, tail, etc).

speed

directness

4. Resting where

   in what position

5. Shelter making (describe or sketch nest, burrow, web, cocoon, etc).

6. Enemies and means of defense.

7. Other activities.

Beneficial or injurious to man and why.

NOTES ON LIVING INSECTS

Date: See picture, plate_____   Measurements:

                                                        Length:
Name of Insect:

                                                        Expanse:

(Underscore such words as apply)

I. Stages Found   Where Found   Number found together

   adult

   pups

   larva or nymph

   eggs

2. Feeding where

   on what

   in what manner

3. Moving about how (walking, swimming, flying etc).

Using what parts (legs, wings, tail, etc).

speed

directness

4. Resting where

   in what position

5. Shelter making (describe or sketch nest, burrow, web, cocoon, etc).

6. Enemies and means of defense.

7. Other activities.

Beneficial or injurious to man and why.

NOTES ON LIVING INSECTS

Date: See picture, plate_____   Measurements:

Name of Insect: Length:

                                       Expanse:

(Underscore such words as apply)

I. Stages Found   Where Found   Number found together

    adult

    pups

    larva or nymph

    eggs

2. Feeding where

    on what

    in what manner

3. Moving about how (walking, swimming, flying etc).

Using what parts (legs, wings, tail, etc).

speed

directness

4. Resting where

   in what position

5. Shelter making (describe or sketch nest, burrow, web, cocoon, etc).

6. Enemies and means of defense.

7. Other activities.

Beneficial or injurious to man and why.

NOTES ON LIVING INSECTS

Date: See picture, plate_____   Measurements:

Name of Insect: Length:

                                          Expanse:

(Underscore such words as apply)

I. Stages Found   Where Found   Number found together

    adult

    pups

    larva or nymph

    eggs

2. Feeding where

    on what

    in what manner

3. Moving about how (walking, swimming, flying etc).

Using what parts (legs, wings, tail, etc).

speed

directness

4. Resting where

   in what position

5. Shelter making (describe or sketch nest, burrow, web, cocoon, etc).

6. Enemies and means of defense.

7. Other activities.

Beneficial or injurious to man and why.

NOTES ON LIVING INSECTS

Date: See picture, plate_____   Measurements:

Name of Insect: Length:

                                                     Expanse:

(Underscore such words as apply)

I. Stages Found   Where Found   Number found together

adult

pups

larva or nymph

eggs

2. Feeding where

on what

in what manner

3. Moving about how (walking, swimming, flying etc).

Using what parts (legs, wings, tail, etc).

speed

directness

4. Resting where

   in what position

5. Shelter making (describe or sketch nest, burrow, web, cocoon, etc).

6. Enemies and means of defense.

7. Other activities.

Beneficial or injurious to man and why.

NOTES ON LIVING INSECTS

Date: See picture, plate_____   Measurements:

Name of Insect: Length:

                                                     Expanse:

(Underscore such words as apply)

I. Stages Found   Where Found   Number found together

   adult

   pups

   larva or nymph

   eggs

2. Feeding where

   on what

   in what manner

3. Moving about how (walking, swimming, flying etc).

Using what parts (legs, wings, tail, etc).

speed

directness

4. Resting where

   in what position

5. Shelter making (describe or sketch nest, burrow, web, cocoon, etc).

6. Enemies and means of defense.

7. Other activities.

Beneficial or injurious to man and why.

NOTES ON LIVING INSECTS

Date: See picture, plate_____   Measurements:

Name of Insect: Length:

                                                 Expanse:

(Underscore such words as apply)

I. Stages Found   Where Found   Number found together

    adult

    pups

    larva or nymph

    eggs

2. Feeding where

    on what

    in what manner

3. Moving about how (walking, swimming, flying etc).

Using what parts (legs, wings, tail, etc).

speed

directness

4. Resting where

   in what position

5. Shelter making (describe or sketch nest, burrow, web, cocoon, etc).

6. Enemies and means of defense.

7. Other activities.

Beneficial or injurious to man and why.

NOTES ON LIVING INSECTS

Date: See picture, plate_____   Measurements:

Name of Insect: Length:

                                  Expanse:

(Underscore such words as apply)

I. Stages Found   Where Found   Number found together

adult

pups

larva or nymph

eggs

2. Feeding where

    on what

    in what manner

3. Moving about how (walking, swimming, flying etc).

Using what parts (legs, wings, tail, etc).

speed

directness

4. Resting where

   in what position

5. Shelter making (describe or sketch nest, burrow, web, cocoon, etc).

6. Enemies and means of defense.

7. Other activities.

Beneficial or injurious to man and why.

NOTES ON LIVING INSECTS

Date: See picture, plate_____   Measurements:

Name of Insect: Length:

                                            Expanse:

(Underscore such words as apply)

I. Stages Found   Where Found   Number found together

    adult

    pups

    larva or nymph

    eggs

2. Feeding where

    on what

    in what manner

3. Moving about how (walking, swimming, flying etc).

Using what parts (legs, wings, tail, etc).

speed

directness

4. Resting where

   in what position

5. Shelter making (describe or sketch nest, burrow, web, cocoon, etc).

6. Enemies and means of defense.

7. Other activities.

Beneficial or injurious to man and why.

NOTES ON LIVING INSECTS

Date: See picture, plate_____ Measurements:

Name of Insect: Length:

Expanse:

(Underscore such words as apply)

I. Stages Found Where Found Number found together

adult

pups

larva or nymph

eggs

2. Feeding where

on what

in what manner

3. Moving about how (walking, swimming, flying etc).

Using what parts (legs, wings, tail, etc).

speed

directness

4. Resting where

   in what position

5. Shelter making (describe or sketch nest, burrow, web, cocoon, etc).

6. Enemies and means of defense.

7. Other activities.

Beneficial or injurious to man and why.

NOTES ON LIVING INSECTS

Date: See picture, plate_____   Measurements:

Name of Insect: Length:

                                                          Expanse:

(Underscore such words as apply)

I. Stages Found   Where Found   Number found together

   adult

   pups

   larva or nymph

   eggs

2. Feeding where

   on what

   in what manner

3. Moving about how (walking, swimming, flying etc).

Using what parts (legs, wings, tail, etc).

speed

directness

4. Resting where

in what position

5. Shelter making (describe or sketch nest, burrow, web, cocoon, etc).

6. Enemies and means of defense.

7. Other activities.

Beneficial or injurious to man and why.

NOTES ON LIVING INSECTS

Date: See picture, plate_____   Measurements:

Name of Insect: Length:

                                                         Expanse:

(Underscore such words as apply)

I. Stages Found   Where Found   Number found together

  adult

  pups

  larva or nymph

  eggs

2. Feeding where

   on what

   in what manner

3. Moving about how (walking, swimming, flying etc).

Using what parts (legs, wings, tail, etc).

speed

directness

4. Resting where

    in what position

5. Shelter making (describe or sketch nest, burrow, web, cocoon, etc).

6. Enemies and means of defense.

7. Other activities.

Beneficial or injurious to man and why.

NOTES ON LIVING INSECTS

Date: See picture, plate_____   Measurements:

Name of Insect: Length:

            Expanse:

(Underscore such words as apply)

I. Stages Found   Where Found   Number found together

adult

pups

larva or nymph

eggs

2. Feeding where

on what

in what manner

3. Moving about how (walking, swimming, flying etc).

Using what parts (legs, wings, tail, etc).

speed

directness

4. Resting where

  in what position

5. Shelter making (describe or sketch nest, burrow, web, cocoon, etc).

6. Enemies and means of defense.

7. Other activities.

Beneficial or injurious to man and why.

NOTES ON LIVING INSECTS

Date: See picture, plate_____   Measurements:

Name of Insect: Length:

                                                Expanse:

(Underscore such words as apply)

I. Stages Found   Where Found   Number found together

adult

pups

larva or nymph

eggs

2. Feeding where

on what

in what manner

3. Moving about how (walking, swimming, flying etc).

Using what parts (legs, wings, tail, etc).

speed

directness

4. Resting where

    in what position

5. Shelter making (describe or sketch nest, burrow, web, cocoon, etc).

6. Enemies and means of defense.

7. Other activities.

Beneficial or injurious to man and why.

NOTES ON LIVING INSECTS

Date: See picture, plate_____   Measurements:

Name of Insect: Length:

                                                     Expanse:

(Underscore such words as apply)

I. Stages Found   Where Found   Number found together

    adult

    pups

    larva or nymph

    eggs

2. Feeding where

    on what

    in what manner

3. Moving about how (walking, swimming, flying etc).

Using what parts (legs, wings, tail, etc).

speed

directness

4. Resting where

   in what position

5. Shelter making (describe or sketch nest, burrow, web, cocoon, etc).

6. Enemies and means of defense.

7. Other activities.

Beneficial or injurious to man and why.

NOTES ON LIVING INSECTS

Date: See picture, plate_____   Measurements:

Name of Insect: Length:

                                                 Expanse:

(Underscore such words as apply)

I. Stages Found   Where Found   Number found together

   adult

   pups

   larva or nymph

   eggs

2. Feeding where

   on what

   in what manner

3. Moving about how (walking, swimming, flying etc).

Using what parts (legs, wings, tail, etc).

speed

directness

4. Resting where

   in what position

5. Shelter making (describe or sketch nest, burrow, web, cocoon, etc).

6. Enemies and means of defense.

7. Other activities.

Beneficial or injurious to man and why.

NOTES ON LIVING INSECTS

Date: See picture, plate_____   Measurements:

Name of Insect: Length:

                                                   Expanse:

(Underscore such words as apply)

I. Stages Found   Where Found   Number found together

adult

pups

larva or nymph

eggs

2. Feeding where

on what

in what manner

3. Moving about how (walking, swimming, flying etc).

Using what parts (legs, wings, tail, etc).

speed

directness

4. Resting where

    in what position

5. Shelter making (describe or sketch nest, burrow, web, cocoon, etc).

6. Enemies and means of defense.

7. Other activities.

Beneficial or injurious to man and why.

NOTES ON LIVING INSECTS

Date: See picture, plate_____   Measurements:

Name of Insect: Length:

                                                          Expanse:

(Underscore such words as apply)

I. Stages Found   Where Found   Number found together

   adult

   pups

   larva or nymph

   eggs

2. Feeding where

   on what

   in what manner

3. Moving about how (walking, swimming, flying etc).

Using what parts (legs, wings, tail, etc).

speed

directness

4. Resting where

   in what position

5. Shelter making (describe or sketch nest, burrow, web, cocoon, etc).

6. Enemies and means of defense.

7. Other activities.

   Beneficial or injurious to man and why.

NOTES ON LIVING INSECTS

Date: See picture, plate_____   Measurements:

                                                       Length:
Name of Insect:

                                                       Expanse:

(Underscore such words as apply)

I. Stages Found   Where Found   Number found together

    adult

    pups

    larva or nymph

    eggs

2. Feeding where

    on what

    in what manner

3. Moving about how (walking, swimming, flying etc).

Using what parts (legs, wings, tail, etc).

speed

directness

4. Resting where

    in what position

5. Shelter making (describe or sketch nest, burrow, web, cocoon, etc).

6. Enemies and means of defense.

7. Other activities.

Beneficial or injurious to man and why.

NOTES ON LIVING INSECTS

Date: See picture, plate_____   Measurements:

                                                     Length:
Name of Insect:

                                                     Expanse:

(Underscore such words as apply)

I. Stages Found   Where Found   Number found together

    adult

    pups

    larva or nymph

    eggs

2. Feeding where

    on what

    in what manner

3. Moving about how (walking, swimming, flying etc).

Using what parts (legs, wings, tail, etc).

speed

directness

4. Resting where

   in what position

5. Shelter making (describe or sketch nest, burrow, web, cocoon, etc).

6. Enemies and means of defense.

7. Other activities.

Beneficial or injurious to man and why.

NOTES ON LIVING INSECTS

Date: See picture, plate_____   Measurements:

Name of Insect: Length:

                                                           Expanse:

(Underscore such words as apply)

I. Stages Found   Where Found   Number found together

   adult

   pups

   larva or nymph

   eggs

2. Feeding where

   on what

   in what manner

3. Moving about how (walking, swimming, flying etc).

Using what parts (legs, wings, tail, etc).

speed

directness

4. Resting where

    in what position

5. Shelter making (describe or sketch nest, burrow, web, cocoon, etc).

6. Enemies and means of defense.

7. Other activities.

Beneficial or injurious to man and why.

NOTES ON LIVING INSECTS

Date: See picture, plate_____   Measurements:

Name of Insect: Length:

                                      Expanse:

(Underscore such words as apply)

I. Stages Found	Where Found	Number found together
adult		
pups		
larva or nymph		
eggs		

2. Feeding where

    on what

    in what manner

3. Moving about how (walking, swimming, flying etc).

Using what parts (legs, wings, tail, etc).

speed

directness

4. Resting where

   in what position

5. Shelter making (describe or sketch nest, burrow, web, cocoon, etc).

6. Enemies and means of defense.

7. Other activities.

Beneficial or injurious to man and why.

LIFE HISTORY RECORD

Name of Insect: See picture, plate_____

I. *Eggs,*

    I. Where laid

    2. How clustered (sketch)

    3. How protected

    4. Shape of egg. (Sketch)   color   size

    5. Hatching: describe how the young comes out.

       time required   date

II. *Larva* or Nymph:

For habits see page_____   See picture, plate_____

I. Molting (describe how skin is shed, time required, etc).

2. Length of larval life (give dates)

3. Number of molts (give dates)

III. *Pupa,*   color

    I. Size

    2. Where found

    3. Nature of pupal life (give dates)

    4. Length of pupal life (give dates)

IV. *Adult Insects,*

    I. Emergence, date observed   Time required

    2. Form changes

    3. Color changes

Summary: Dates of egg laying:

of transformation to pupa: of hatching:

number reared: to adult:

LIFE HISTORY RECORD

Name of Insect: See picture, plate_____

I. *Eggs,*

    I. Where laid

    2. How clustered (sketch)

    3. How protected

    4. Shape of egg. (Sketch)   color   size

    5. Hatching: describe how the young comes out.

      time required   date

II. *Larva* or Nymph:

For habits see page_____   See picture, plate_____

I. Molting (describe how skin is shed, time required, etc).

2. Length of larval life (give dates)

3. Number of molts (give dates)

III. *Pupa,*   color

    I. Size

    2. Where found

    3. Nature of pupal life (give dates)

    4. Length of pupal life (give dates)

IV. *Adult Insects,*

    I. Emergence, date observed   Time required

    2. Form changes

    3. Color changes

Summary: Dates of egg laying:

of transformation to pupa: of hatching:

number reared: to adult:

LIFE HISTORY RECORD

Name of Insect: See picture, plate_____

I. *Eggs,*

    I. Where laid

    2. How clustered (sketch)

    3. How protected

    4. Shape of egg. (Sketch)   color   size

    5. Hatching: describe how the young comes out.

        time required   date

II. *Larva* or Nymph:

For habits see page_____   See picture, plate_____

I. Molting (describe how skin is shed, time required, etc).

2. Length of larval life (give dates)

3. Number of molts (give dates)

III. *Pupa,*   color

    1. Size

    2. Where found

    3. Nature of pupal life (give dates)

    4. Length of pupal life (give dates)

IV. *Adult Insects,*

    1. Emergence, date observed   Time required

    2. Form changes

    3. Color changes

Summary: Dates of egg laying:

of transformation to pupa: of hatching:

number reared: to adult:

LIFE HISTORY RECORD

Name of Insect: See picture, plate_____

I. *Eggs,*

    I. Where laid

    2. How clustered (sketch)

    3. How protected

    4. Shape of egg. (Sketch)   color   size

    5. Hatching: describe how the young comes out.

        time required   date

II. *Larva* or Nymph:

For habits see page_____   See picture, plate_____

I. Molting (describe how skin is shed, time required, etc).

2. Length of larval life (give dates)

3. Number of molts (give dates)

III. *Pupa,*   color

    I. Size

    2. Where found

    3. Nature of pupal life (give dates)

    4. Length of pupal life (give dates)

IV. *Adult Insects,*

    I. Emergence, date observed   Time required

    2. Form changes

    3. Color changes

Summary: Dates of egg laying:

of transformation to pupa: of hatching:

number reared: to adult:

LIFE HISTORY RECORD

Name of Insect: See picture, plate_____

I. *Eggs,*

    I. Where laid

    2. How clustered (sketch)

    3. How protected

    4. Shape of egg. (Sketch)   color   size

    5. Hatching: describe how the young comes out.

       time required   date

II. *Larva* or Nymph:

For habits see page_____   See picture, plate_____

I. Molting (describe how skin is shed, time required, etc).

2. Length of larval life (give dates)

3. Number of molts (give dates)

III. *Pupa,* color

    I. Size

    2. Where found

    3. Nature of pupal life (give dates)

    4. Length of pupal life (give dates)

IV. *Adult Insects,*

    I. Emergence, date observed   Time required

    2. Form changes

    3. Color changes

Summary: Dates of egg laying:

of transformation to pupa: of hatching:

number reared: to adult:

LIFE HISTORY RECORD

Name of Insect: See picture, plate_____

I. *Eggs,*

    I. Where laid

    2. How clustered (sketch)

    3. How protected

    4. Shape of egg. (Sketch)   color   size

    5. Hatching: describe how the young comes out.

        time required   date

II. *Larva* or Nymph:

For habits see page_____   See picture, plate_____

I. Molting (describe how skin is shed, time required, etc).

2. Length of larval life (give dates)

3. Number of molts (give dates)

III. *Pupa,*   color

    I. Size

    2. Where found

    3. Nature of pupal life (give dates)

    4. Length of pupal life (give dates)

IV. *Adult Insects,*

    I. Emergence, date observed   Time required

    2. Form changes

    3. Color changes

Summary: Dates of egg laying:

of transformation to pupa: of hatching:

number reared: to adult:

Insects

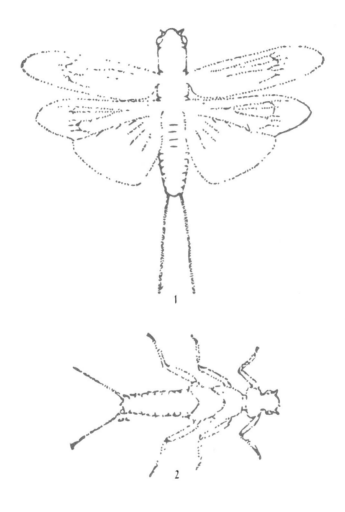

Stone-fly

1. Adult.   2. Nymph

Plate 1
See Page _____

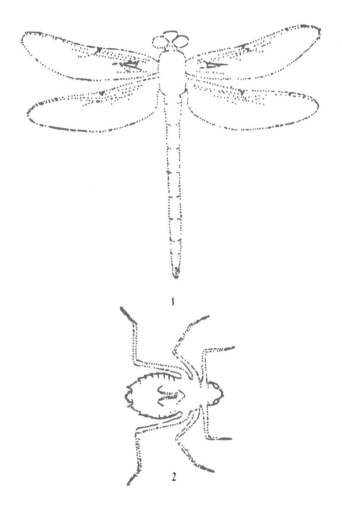

Dragon-fly

1. Adult. 2. Nymph

Plate 2
See Page _____

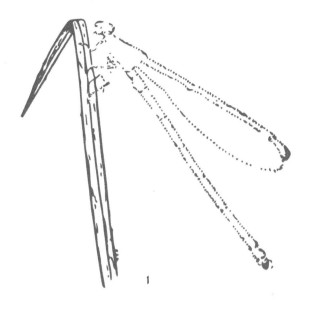

Damsel-fly

1. Adult.   2. Nymph

Plate 3
See Page _____

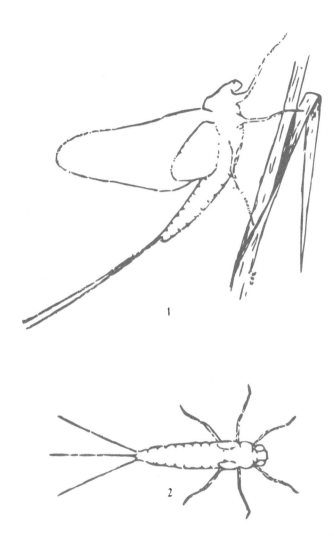

May-fly

1. Adult.   2. Nymph

Plate 4
See Page _____

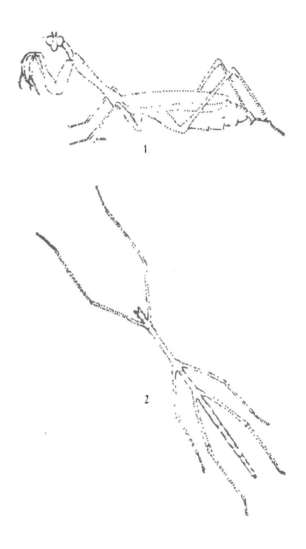

Orthoptera

1. Mantis   2. A Walking Stick

Plate 5
See Page _____

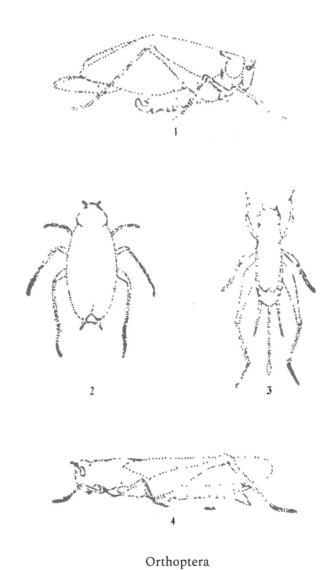

Orthoptera

1. Katydid   2. A Cockroach   3. A Cricket   4. A Grasshopper

Plate 6
See Page _____

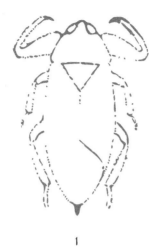

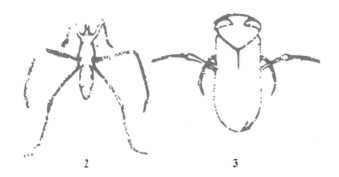

Aquatic Hemiptera

1. Giant Water-bug   2. Water-strider   3. A Water-boatman

Plate 7
See Page _____

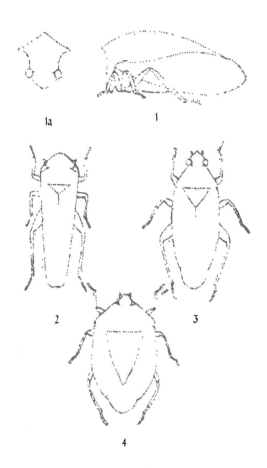

Leaf-inhabiting Hemiptera
1. A Treehopper   *1a.* Face view   2. A Leaf-hopper
4. A Leaf-bug   5. A Stink-bug

Plate 8
See Page _____

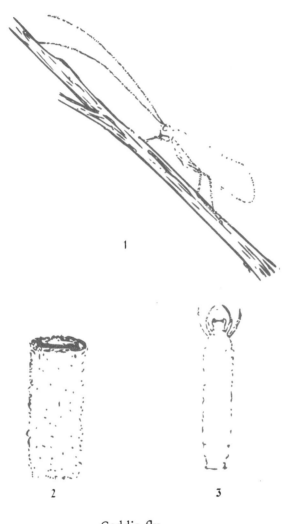

1

2   3

Caddis-fly

1. Adult   2. A Case   3. Larva

Plate 9
See Page _____

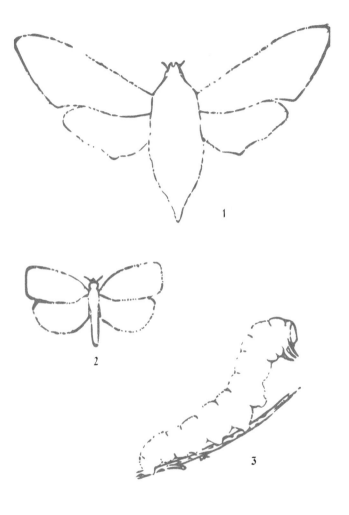

Moths

1. Hawk-moth   2. Tineid-moth   3. Hawk-moth Larva

Plate 10
See Page _____

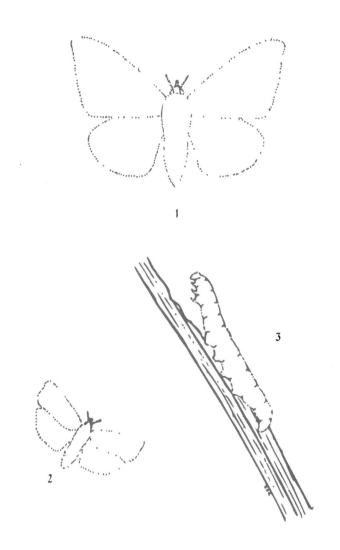

Moths

1. Owlet-moth   2. Tortricid-moth   3. Owlet-moth Larva

Plate 11
See Page _____

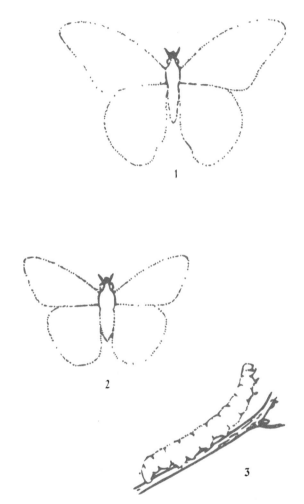

Butterflies

1. Monarch Butterfly   2. Slipper-butterfly   3. Butterfly larva

Plate 12
See Page _____

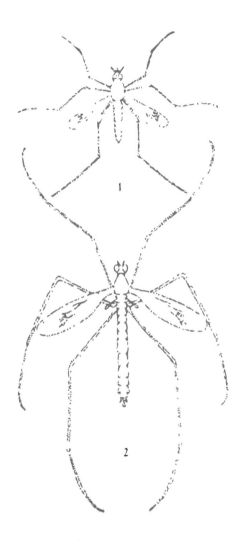

Diptera

1. A Mosquito   2. A Crane-fly

Plate 13
See Page _____

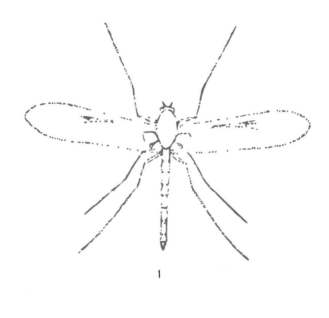

1

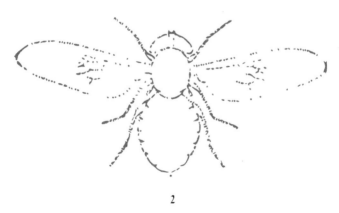

2

Diptera

1. A Midge   2. A Horse-fly

Plate 14
See Page _____

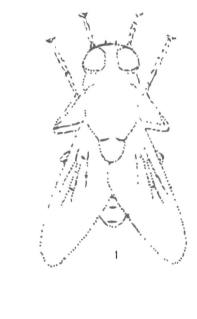

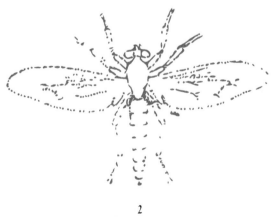

Diptera

1. House-fly   2. A Robber-fly

Plate 15
See Page _____

1

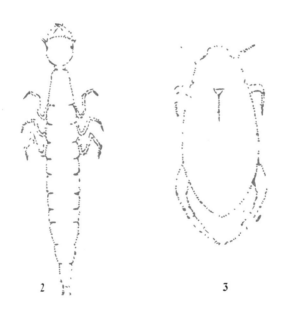

2   3

Water Beetles
1. A Whirligig-beetle   2. Diving-beetle Larva.
3. Adult Diving Beetle

Plate 16
See Page _____

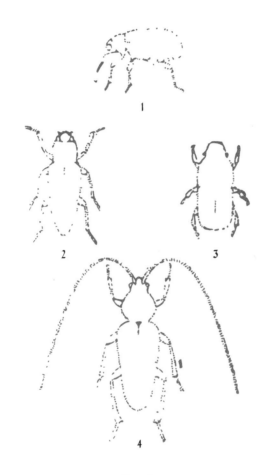

Beetles
1. A Weevil   2. Buprestid Beetle   3. Engraver-beetle
4. Long-horned Beetle

Plate 17
See Page _____

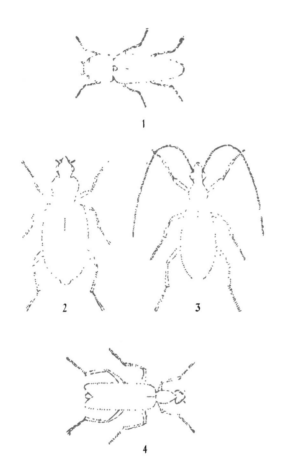

Beetles
1. A Click-beetle 2. Ground-beetle 3. Tiger-beetle
4. Blister-beetle

Plate 18
See Page _____

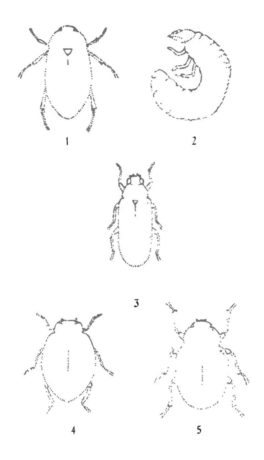

Beetles
1. May-beetle   2. May-beetle larva   3. Leaf-beetle
4. Lady-bird-beetle   5. Potato-beetle

Plate 19
See Page _____

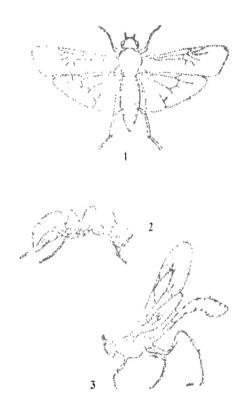

Hymenoptera
1. Sawfly 2. An Ant 3. An Ichneumonfly

Plate 20
See Page _____

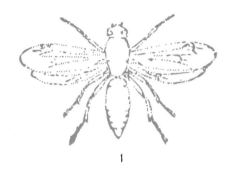

1

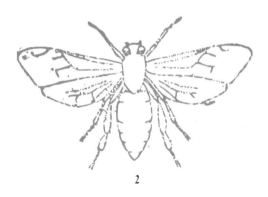

2

Hymenoptera
1. A Bee   2. A Wasp

Plate 21
See Page _____

INDEX TO PICTURES

CPSIA information can be obtained
at www.ICGtesting.com
Printed in the USA
LVHW092131130621
690142LV00016B/505